Water Wise

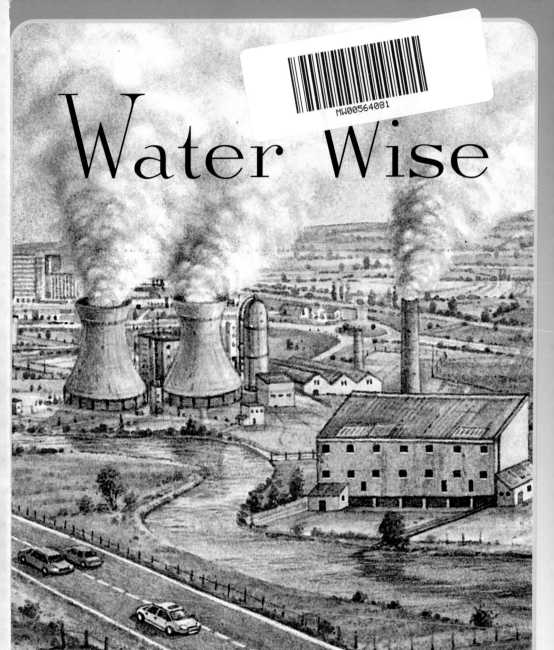

Contents

Features

Is it a solid? Is it a gas? Is it a liquid? See if you can identify the different forms of water in the photo on page 9.

Where does the water go when you pull the plug on your bath? Find out in **Down the Drain** on page 13.

How do you get the water you need to brush your teeth in the morning? Find out how people in many different countries get their water supplies on page 15.

Industry's need for water sometimes pollutes wetland habitats. Find out about an environmental disaster in Spain on page 25.

Why can some insects walk on water?
Visit www.rigbyinfoquest.com
for more about WATER.

Water, water everywhere
and all the boards did shrink;
Water, water everywhere.
Nor any drop to drink.

Long ago, sailors were stuck in the middle of the ocean if there was no wind. Their ships had no engines, so they had to wait until the wind blew again. These sailors often ran out of freshwater. They were surrounded by water that they could not drink.

A Lack of Water

Three-fourths of Earth's surface is water, but most of it is salty. Only 1% of all the water on Earth is available to us for use. One of the greatest problems facing Earth in the twenty-first century is a lack of water. Today, Earth's population is about 6 billion. By 2050, the population of Earth is expected to be 9 billion, yet the amount of freshwater is not increasing.

The World's Water

- 97% of Earth's water is salty.
- 2% of Earth's water is frozen at the polar caps and in glaciers.
- 1% is available for drinking, household use, irrigation, and industry.

And every tongue, through utter drought,
Was withered at the root;
We could not speak, no more than if
We had been choked with soot.

With no rain in sight, sailors soon ran out
of drinking water and their bodies would begin
to dehydrate.

H₂O

All living things need water. In fact, the bodies of most living things are made up mostly of water. Several times a day, our bodies must take in a chemical called hydrogen oxide. Hydrogen oxide is the chemical name for water. We call it H_2O for short.

Water may seem ordinary to us, but it has properties that no other substance has. It can dissolve other substances. Over time, it can wear away rock. When it is frozen, it can split rocks apart.

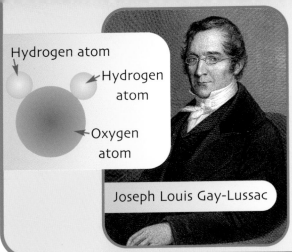

Hydrogen atom

Hydrogen atom

Oxygen atom

Joseph Louis Gay-Lussac

An Important Discovery

In 1805, Joseph Louis Gay-Lussac, a French scientist, and Alexander von Humboldt, a German scientist, discovered that water contains two volumes of hydrogen for every volume of oxygen. That's why the chemical symbol for water is H_2O.

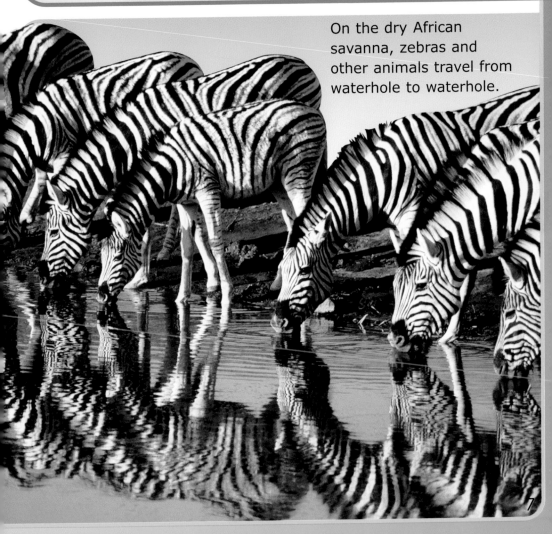

On the dry African savanna, zebras and other animals travel from waterhole to waterhole.

Pure water has no color, taste, or smell. It comes in many different forms. It can be hail, ice, frost, or snow. It can be mist or steam or rain.

Water can change its state between liquid, gas, or solid. These changes are necessary to life on Earth. For example, if water could not change from gas to liquid, there would be no rain.

IN FOCUS

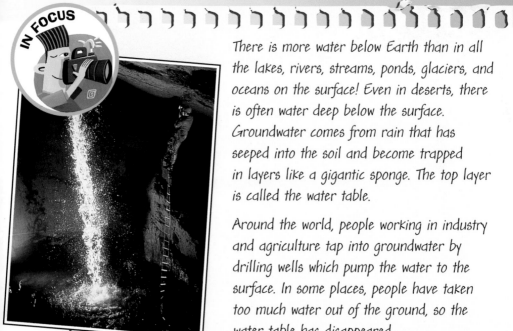

There is more water below Earth than in all the lakes, rivers, streams, ponds, glaciers, and oceans on the surface! Even in deserts, there is often water deep below the surface. Groundwater comes from rain that has seeped into the soil and become trapped in layers like a gigantic sponge. The top layer is called the water table.

Around the world, people working in industry and agriculture tap into groundwater by drilling wells which pump the water to the surface. In some places, people have taken too much water out of the ground, so the water table has disappeared.

FACT FINDER

Water has three states—liquid, solid, and gas.
Where do you see each state in this photo?

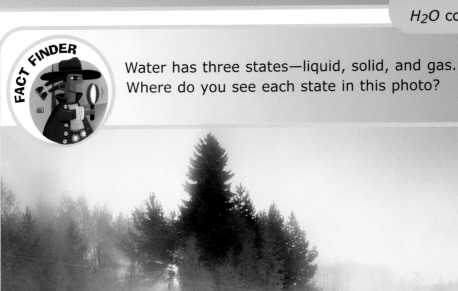

SITESEEING · WATER, EARTH, & SKY ·

Why can some insects walk on water?

Visit www.rigbyinfoquest.com
for more about **WATER.**

My lips were wet, my throat was cold,
My garments were all dank;
Sure I had drunken in my dreams,
And still my body drank.

(From *The Rime of the Ancient Mariner* by Samuel Taylor Coleridge)

Rain eventually did come. The ancient mariner survived to tell his tale. Samuel Taylor Coleridge wrote this famous poem more than two hundred years ago.

Waiting for Rain

Today, many people around the world wait anxiously for rain. Rain replaces Earth's 1% of usable water. It fills streams, rivers, lakes, ponds, and dams. It freshens baked fields and makes crops grow.

Rain comes and goes all over the planet, but it never disappears because the water cycle is a "closed system." This means that the same water falls as rain over and over again. Water that fell as rain millions of years ago is still falling on us today! The reason water keeps circulating is that it can change its state from gas to liquid and back again.

World Rainfall Map

Key to Rainfall

Average Number of Inches per Year

- more than 60
- 40–60
- 20–40
- 10–20
- less than 10 inches

Scientists spend a lot of time and energy working out ways to bring water into dry areas.

Safe to Drink

Supplying clean water to people's homes is a huge task. In most cities and towns, water is collected from sources such as rivers, lakes, and groundwater to be stored in **reservoirs** or dams. The water is then filtered, purified, and pumped through a vast network of pipes to our homes.

After water has been used, it is collected and treated before it is returned to rivers or the ocean.

Down the Drain

Pipes deliver clean water to our homes and industries, and drains take used water away from them. Wastewater flows into a pipe and is carried to a water-treatment plant. At the plant, the wastewater is sifted to remove solid materials. It is then left to settle in tanks, where special bacteria and other useful microorganisms feed on the waste. The treated water is then let out into rivers, lakes, or oceans and becomes part of the water cycle again.

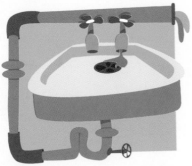

1. Wastewater is carried away from homes and factories by pipes.

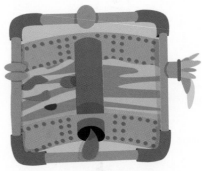

2. The wastewater is sifted to remove solid materials.

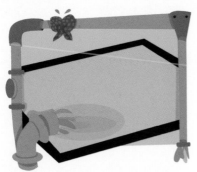

3. The wastewater is left in tanks, where microorganisms feed on the waste.

4. The treated water is sometimes used to irrigate golf courses or gardens.

13

Dirty Water

Not all of Earth's 6 billion people get clean water to drink. Bacteria from poor **sanitation** can make water deadly, and yet over 1.2 billion people drink unclean water. Each year, over 5 million people die from waterborne diseases such as cholera. Chemicals from industry and agriculture often pollute lakes, rivers, and streams, too.

Rivers are a vital source of life for many communities, but the water may no longer be fit to drink when the rivers are heavily used for everything from washing to irrigation and industry.

Keeping the world's water supply safe to drink is a huge job. Scientists around the world are constantly working on ways to improve the quality and supply of water.

FAST FACTS

In many places around the world, people have to walk long distances to collect water and carry it to their homes.

Drip irrigation is best because no water is lost through evaporation.

Every Drop Counts

Water for Agriculture

Through irrigation systems, agriculture uses 70% of all Earth's usable freshwater. In many parts of the world, irrigation methods are wasteful of water because much of the water is lost through **evaporation** before it ever reaches the crops.

Because of irrigation systems, once-mighty rivers such as the Nile in Egypt and the Colorado in the United States have been reduced to trickles before they reach the sea. Some no longer reach the sea at all.

Getting the most from each drop of water is important on our thirsty planet, so scientists are working on less wasteful ways to irrigate land. Drip irrigation uses 70% less water than other methods. Tubes with small holes take water to the roots of the plants.

Sprinkler systems keep crops irrigated, but they waste a lot of water.

Sharing Water Resources

The need for water increases as populations grow larger. In many places, getting fresh drinking water is a constant problem. This can make water a source of conflict. Many countries and states share rivers with their neighbors, so arguments over water rights and water usage are common.

Damming a river to provide water and power for some people may mean that people farther downstream lose much of their water. Water pollution is also a big problem. In some places, pollution from sewage systems, industries, and farms runs into rivers. Some people even dump garbage into rivers. This pollution flows downstream and spoils the water for the people who live farther down the river.

The Colorado River provides water for cities and farms in seven states of the United States and an area of Mexico. Its course is controlled by many dams, canals, and pumping stations.

Trash chokes this waterway in Bangladesh, polluting it for every person and animal that needs it.

The Great Lakes

The Great Lakes of North America—Lake Superior, Lake Michigan, Lake Huron, Lake Erie, and Lake Ontario—along with the rivers and streams and small lakes that feed and drain them, are the world's largest surface area of freshwater. This area covers 94,000 square miles.

The water cycle controls the water level of the lakes. The first half of the cycle begins in the clouds. Rain and snow fall onto the lakes and the **watershed.**

The second half of the cycle takes water away through evaporation from the surface of the lakes and **transpiration** from plants growing in the watershed.

The Water Cycle

1. Moisture is released from clouds as rain, hail, or snow.

2. Rain runs into lakes and rivers.

6. Water vapor condenses to form clouds.

5. Water evaporates.

5. Plants transpire.

3. Rain soaks into underground pools and rivers.

4. Rivers flow into the sea.

5. Water evaporates.

21

If rain and runoff from the watershed is less than the loss of water due to evaporation, transpiration, and river flow, then the levels of the lakes drop. Lake levels have dropped dramatically in the last ten years.

Global Warming

Over the last 100 years, Earth has warmed about one degree Fahrenheit. Some scientists believe that Earth is getting warmer on its own, but many scientists believe that Earth is getting warmer because of air pollution. Effects of global warming may include droughts and also flooding as melting glaciers raise sea levels. Scientists are studying these possible effects.

Air temperatures have been warmer, and there has been less rain and snow in the watershed. The lakes have not frozen in the winter, so there has been a longer time for evaporation to occur. Some scientists believe global warming can be blamed for these warmer temperatures and the drop in the lakes' levels.

Sandbars appearing in Lake Huron, Michigan, show how low the water levels have dropped.

Water and Industry

Without water, many industries would grind to a halt. Factories use water to manufacture raw materials into many products we use, such as clothes, paper, food, and drink. Some products, such as plastic and steel, are "thirsty" products that use a lot of water.

Water is also used to produce electricity. The energy in steam and in falling water is used to turn turbines that make electricity. In less than the hundred years since electricity was discovered, people have changed the shape of rivers, and valleys have been flooded for hydroelectric systems. Dams, locks, power plants, pipes, and canals put water to work.

Papermaking

It takes a lot of water to make paper, so paper mills are usually beside rivers, like this one on the Gold River in British Columbia, Canada.

Wood is broken down into tiny fibers and mixed with water. When the water is drained, a layer of pulp remains. This pulp is dried to produce paper.

EARTH WATCH

Industry can cause wetland pollution. The Donana on the Atlantic coast of Spain are the country's largest wetlands. Millions of migratory birds stop there each year. In 1998, these wetlands suffered a disaster when a reservoir of poisonous water from a zinc mine burst and flooded the Donana. Many thousands of fish and birds died, and about 12,000 acres of orchards, rice fields, and cotton plantations were coated with toxic black mud. Despite a successful cleanup, the Donana wetlands are still recovering today.

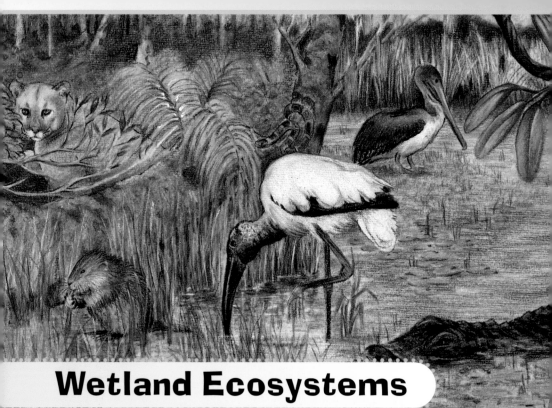

Wetland Ecosystems

A wetland is an area of land that is covered by water for some or all of the year. Wetlands are important ecosystems that are threatened by people's demand for water. They are homes to many special plants and animals that are not found anywhere else.

The Everglades in Florida is a rich wetland that is under threat. So much water is drawn off to meet the needs of people that the number of birds and other animals living there has dropped. Water pollution is also a problem. People are working to restore the Everglades, but it will take a long time.

Key to Illustration

Florida

1. Florida panther
2. Coral snake
3. Pelican
4. Spoonbill
5. Green anole
6. Muskrat
7. Wood stork
8. Raccoon
9. Alligator
10. Tree snail
11. Snapping turtle
12. Manatee

Water Wise or Wasteful?

FACT FINDER

Spot the pressure water is under. Where can you see water being wasted or polluted? Where can you see water being used wisely?

Turn to page 30 for the answers.

28

Water Wise or Wasteful?

1. Electricity generation WISE
2. Dam WISE
3. Spray irrigation WASTEFUL
4. Trough for stock WISE
5. Barrels leaking into the river WASTEFUL
6. Drip irrigation WISE
7. Fishing WISE
8. Littering WASTEFUL
9. Industrial waste going straight into the river WASTEFUL
10. Swimming in a pool WISE
11. Drinking bottled water WISE
12. Uncontrolled stock damaging the riverbank WASTEFUL
13. Kayaking WISE
14. Pollution of the wetland habitat WASTEFUL
15. Watering the garden in the heat of the day WASTEFUL
16. Leaking hose WASTEFUL
17. Leaking tap WASTEFUL
18. Running water while cleaning teeth WASTEFUL

Glossary

dehydrate – to not have enough water in the body. All living creatures need water so that they do not become dehydrated.

evaporation – the process by which water changes into a vapor or a gas

reservoir – a natural or purpose-built holding area for storing a very large amount of water

sanitation – systems for cleaning the water supply and treating sewage. Sanitation helps protect people from disease.

transpiration – the process by which water vapor escapes from a living plant and enters the atmosphere

watershed – sloping land, rivers, and streams draining into a body of water

Index

Research Starters

1 In some places where there is little freshwater, saltwater from the ocean is treated to remove the salt. Find out about the process of desalination.

2 Even in countries where water is not very scarce, saving water is a good idea. Make a list of the ways your family uses water every day for a week. How could your family use less water?

3 Imagine life without hot and cold water on tap. Where do people without plumbing get their water? How did pioneer families cope?

4 Many kinds of birds and animals make their homes by water, but these homes are often threatened by building development. Find out about an endangered wetland animal, such as the Florida panther. What can be done to save it?